Wax Lyrical

Wax Lyrical

A Kinkster's Guide to Wax Play

By
TinderHella

Hella Good House of Publishing

wax lyr-i-cal
v.
1) to talk in a high enthusiastic way
2) to rhapsodize

Copyright © 2018 by TinderHella
All rights reserved. No part of this book may be reproduced in any form or by any electronic or mechanical means including information storage and retrieval systems, without permission in writing from the author. The only exception is by a reviewer, who may quote short excerpts in a review.

All photography by Kevin Gibbs (DFWPhoto.com)
Rope work by TwistedCupcake
Models: Feeling_Frisky, Maraxes, and Raziella
All photos Copyright ©2018 by Jen Bochenko

Cover designed by Angie Alaya (pro_ebookcovers)

HellaMean.com
TinderHella.com

Printed in the United States of America
First Printing: August 2018

Hella Good House of Publishing

ISBN-13: 978-0-9996819-6-1
ISBN-10: 0-9996819-6-1

Dedicated to

Every wax play partner who entrusted me with their safety, both physically and emotionally.

I don't take that responsibility lightly.

But between you and me…I think all of you are nuts!

Thank You

E & E – This is what I've been doing all this time. Don't judge me.

Ella – no one will ever be able to take away the fact that you were my first person on which I ever dripped wax

KB – who asked me to take notes at the first wax play demo and class I ever attended

Maraxes, Feeling Frisky, and Raziella – my beautiful friends and models
Also, thank you to their Daddies, Masters, and Sirs

SB

My inner circle of friends who will exist in my life always (DC, MJ, P007, TR, L, the sisters, to name but a few)

Spectrum

|Q| for saving my ass and my sanity

Table of Contents

Prologue 1

Wax Poetic 2

Safety 3

Safety - Quick List 6

My Wax Scene is Still a Scene and Often Can Still Be Dangerous 7

Types of Wax 10

Wax and Additives Quick Reference 16

Types of Candles 19

Types of Candles Quick Reference 22

Prep 23

Prep - Quick List 25

Style 27

Removal 37

Aftercare 43

About TinderHella 44

Wax Candles Vendors 45

Endnotes 49

Prologue

The last book on wax and temperature play was released in 2004 so it felt like it was time for an update.

Since this book is intended to be used as a basic guide to wax play, the chapters have been kept short and tables and checklists have been added to the end of some.

Pictures were added not just to illustrate the text but also to show the absolute beauty that is wax play.

Each form of BDSM play carry its own inherent risks. While the author has done her best to research the information contained within these pages, this book is still just a basic guideline and readers assume any and all risks when participating in wax play.

TinderHella is not the end all, be all wax expert, so please contact her to address any errors in facts and information.

She follows PRICK.

Personal Responsibility, Informed Consensual Kink

Wax Poetic

(posted to Fetlife Saturday, January 7, 2017)

Your body is my canvas
Your skin my inspiration
And I find peace in your pieces
Giving purpose to my obsession

You hold your breath
as your energy and my energy
becomes our energy

The wax that stings your skin
The same wax I lose myself in
Is the same wax that can
Outwardly express how I feel within

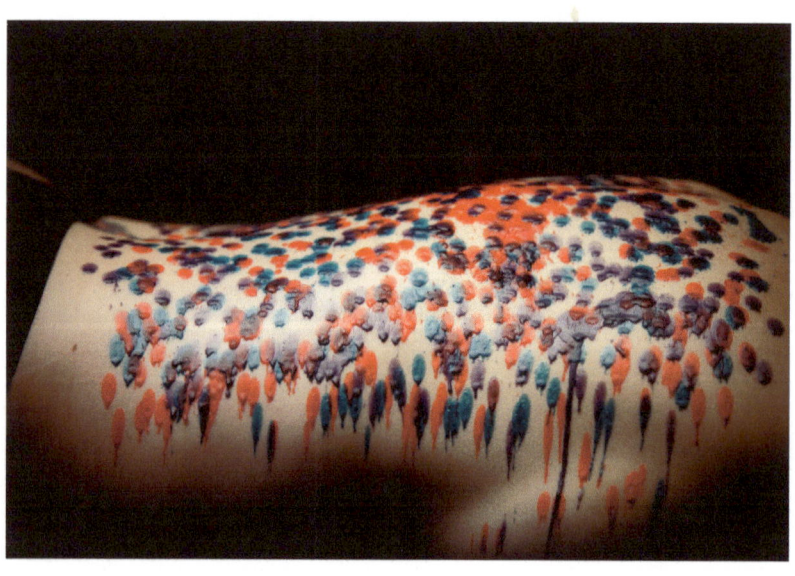

Safety

Whether or not your wax play includes an open flame, it does have its dangers. My goal is to present you with all the possible dangers and complications, so you can best prevent them. With edge play, it is not if but rather when.

Wax that is too hot can cause second-degree burns. According to the American Burn Association, it isn't just the temperature that matters. The length of exposure also factors in. Boiling water scalds immediately. But being exposed to water at 170°F for as little as half a second can also lead to second or even third-degree burns. Water at 150°F can also lead to serious injuries if one is exposed for as little as two seconds.[1]

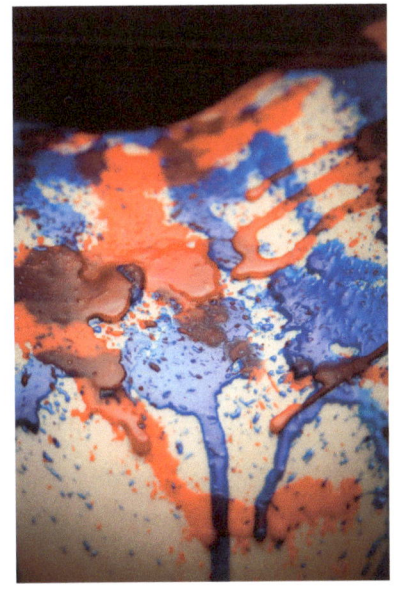

It is important to be aware of these facts because not only is wax hot; wax sticks. So, you might be using a low melting point paraffin candle but allowing it to pool, layering wax atop can still lead to burns.

That is how I was burned. My partner allowed wax (low melting point paraffin) to pool in the small of my back. I called yellow to pause, work through and process the pain, and then we continued because neither of us knew better. I ended up with a quarter sized blister on my back. In pictures you can see exactly where the wax had pooled, insulating the heat, and as a result burned my skin.

Having a wet washcloth or two within reach is very helpful when dealing with a burn or if, heaven forbid, something catches on fire. The cool cloth can help draw the heat away from the body and can also smother flames. If your partner calls red, remove the wax in that area immediately and lay the cloth over the skin. Also, you can lay it over the wax directly to speed the cooling and hardening of the wax, making it easier to remove.

If you are melting your wax in a Crock-Pot, electric skillet, or directly on the stove, be careful not to spill the wax or water all over yourself or your partner. Always prepare enough room on a sturdy flat surface to prevent anything from toppling over.

Using candles presents its own dangers. Candles also need flat sturdy surfaces to prevent a toppling flame from setting fire to the surroundings.[2]

Even if you set your candles on a sturdy surface, loose clothing, drapes, paper, and other lightweight items can be set on fire if they come in direct contact with the flame or even if a few feet above it.

Having set off the smoke detector in my own bedroom, I have found that having a fan indirectly creating an air flow helps prevent false alarms. However direct drafts from air vents or ceiling fans can interfere with a candle burning evenly or even blow lightweight and loose items into it.

Melting or dripping, you should always test the wax on yourself first by dripping some on your inner wrist.

Pets should be locked away during playtime as well. Depending on their level of curiosity they might knock something over or even burn themselves. That's the kind of hot pussy we avoid.

Safety - Quick List

- Fire extinguisher
- Wet towels
- Sturdy flat surface for supplies

Watch for

- Direct air flow
- Loose curtains, drapes, sheets, or pillows
- Loose paper for other lightweight items
- Pets

Remember:

- Listen to your partner
- Test on your wrist first
- Avoid letting the wax pool
- Be aware of layering so wax which can hold the heat against the skin

My Wax Scene is Still a Scene and Often Can Still Be Dangerous

(Posted to Fetlife on Wednesday, April 26, 2017)

I know. Because I've scarred someone.

I've gained a little bit of attention in my local community for topping with wax. Just a bit. A few people may know me. My scenes are extensive and can be elaborate. I like to say:

> Wax isn't part of my scene. Wax IS my scene.

Some say I have developed a passion for wax. I would, however, describe it more like an obsession. I even make my own candles. If you approach me with questions, I can and will talk your ear off.

And I talk a lot about safety. Therein lies my reputation. I take precautions when I play. I try to educate you. I will do nothing to you that I haven't done to myself. Which is why I've given myself 2nd degree burns 3 times on my shins.

When I did the birthday cake featured scene, I didn't just head on into the place and break out the wax. I spent 4 weeks figuring out each step and I fucked up a few times. Testing the process caused me to burn not just myself but also a play partner. I mostly learn what NOT to do when I test play.

So please remember:

Wax IS edge play.

Wax often involves fire and can never be completely safe.

My wax scenes require minions. Minions (spotters) are watching and are prepared for something to go wrong/catch fire. Minions make sure my candles are out before they get set down. Minions intercept lookie loos who might be getting too close.

During a scene I'm usually giggly, chatty, and silly. The seemingly casual appearance seems inviting to the voyeurs, whom I love, but my scene is still a scene and all my energy is focused on my partner. We can chat afterwards.

Don't get me wrong. I know...

Wax is incredibly sexy and fun.
Wax can be sadistic or can be sensual.
Wax can be artistic.

But wax cannot be completely safe so make yourself risk aware.

Since wax is seen more as a sensual scene, too many people don't consider all the aspects of wax play. Consider these questions (not at all a comprehensive list):

What kind of wax are you using?
Are you going to drip or pour?
Where will you drip it?
How will you get it off?

This last question posed such an issue for a friend of mine that he and his girlfriend just went to bed apparently still covered in clumps of wax.

No one should crack whips on someone without practicing. No one should suspend someone without practicing. No one should drip wax on someone without knowing the answers to the questions I listed above. And then some.

Although I jokingly call myself the Mistress of Wax, I hardly seriously consider myself the end all, be all, final say, know everything Wax Goddess.

I encourage everyone to:

- ✓ Read from more than one source
- ✓ Ask questions of more than one person
- ✓ Educate yourself with the knowledge of many

Now pardon me...I'm being nerdy with wax and conducting an experiment.

Types of Wax

Many different waxes are used for making candles and each of these has its own characteristics. An important one of those is melting point. Additives such as scents, oils, and other fillers can affect that melting point average.

Paraffin

Paraffin is derived from petroleum and was found to be an excellent candle making material. It was cheaper to produce and burned more cleanly. Today, paraffin wax is the most commonly used wax for general use candles.[3]

Low melting point paraffin is the most popular wax of all kinky candles and companies proudly advertise 100% paraffin in their products. Be careful though because paraffin doesn't have a single melting point. It has a melting range based on the amount of oil within it. The more refined the paraffin, the less the oil, the harder the resulting wax, and the higher the melting point average.

The paraffin used in standard candles is very hard and brittle because most of the oil has been removed. Spa paraffin has a high oil content which keeps it feeling soft. It also can be mixed with mineral oil and essential oils to lower the melting point.

All of these are 100% paraffin wax. I find it best to compare with dairy products. We call everything from heavy whipping cream to skim milk dairy. However, attempting to make whipped cream from skim milk won't yield the same results. The difference in dairy won't lead to injuries though.

Even if you don't learn the specifics, knowing there is a difference will help prevent injuries. Paraffin can melt at 120°F, but its melting range can go up to and beyond 155°F.[4][5] If you are expecting one and get the other, you might just be completely turned off by both.

Soy

Soy is also a popular wax for wax play. Its low melting point and natural plant source makes it an attractive alternative to paraffin.

Soy candles have become popular partially due to a plant-based source-the soybean. Many believe waxes derived from plants are safer for the environment and make for better candles than paraffin. We'll leave the controversial candle sciences out and focus on the fun.

Soy wax is softer with a melting point average that falls within the lower melting range of paraffin. For those people who are more sensitive when it comes to temperature, 100% soy wax candles are a good way to start. However, allergies to soy should be revealed during negotiations to avoid a bad reaction during the scene. Those with mild allergies should test in a small area first if they still wish to play.

Beeswax

Beeswax is another natural resource renewable wax that is popular in decorative candles. Beeswax as a resource in general has been used for thousands of years; Egyptians used it in the mummification process.[6]

Beeswax, however, is very unsafe having a very high melting point which begins to at 147°F.[7] If you find erotic wax play candles made with beeswax, check the other ingredients. Some shops blend beeswax with other plant-based waxes to avoid using petroleum-based paraffin.

Additives

There are several additives candle-makers use for their candles. All else being equal these additives can increase the melting points to varying degrees.

When it comes to scented candles, so many variables come into play. Type of wax, type of fragrance, and type of additives will all effect the candle's scent throw[8] (how strongly the scent can be detected when both cold and burning). So, while the scent itself may not increase the melting point, companies frequently will use other additives that will.[9]

Stearic Acid (Stearin)

Stearic acid is a wax hardener that has been used in candles for over 150 years. It helps the candles such as tapers keep their shape as well as helped make the colors more vibrant.[10]

Stearin has an average melting point of 158°F which will change the average melting point of the wax it's added to.[11][12]

Vybar

Vybar is an alternative to stearin and is used in paraffin with melting points below 130°F. It is also a hardener that can enhance color and fragrance quality.[13]

Most wax is sold with these two additives already mixed in. This is one of the many reasons using random candles off the shelf is such a gamble and is very unsafe.

DO NOT USE:

Gel candles can be pretty to look at but burn at a very high temperature and will severely injure the skin. They have been known to shatter their glass containers spontaneously.[14][15]

Birthday candles may seem like an alluring option but are actually very dangerous. They are intended to be decorative and use high melting point wax and additives to keep their shapes and colors. Some are wrapped in a plastic coating which when melted can severely burn the skin.

Metallic candles are also frequently wrapped in a plastic coating to give it its sheen.[16][17] As you can see in the picture above, when the candle is burned, the coating doesn't burn away like the wax itself.

Decorative candles should just be avoided completely. They are meant to be attractive in a room and not on the skin.

It is best to stick with candles made especially for erotic wax play and reach out to their manufacturers if you have any questions about their contents. I've added a list of vendors at the end of the book to help get you started.

Wax and Additives Quick Reference

Material	Average Melting Range (°F)	Descriptions
Paraffin	116-147	petroleum product translucent in appearance preferred in candle making
Soy	115-135	plant based milkier appearance often blended with paraffin
Beeswax	147 and up	naturally occurring very hot animal by-product
Gel	180-220	petroleum and polymers too hot known to shatter containers spontaneously
Bayberry	116-120	plant based expensive natural scent and color

Additives

Material	*Average Melting Range (°F)*	*Descriptions*
Stearin/ Stearic Acid	158	wax hardener helps retain and enhance color and scent
Vybar 260 Vybar 103	130 160	wax hardener helps retain and enhance color and scent

Types of Candles

Container candles are very popular. The wax melting in the cup means splashing and pouring instead of one drop at a time. Since the wax does not need to hold its shape, additives used to harden the wax are not needed.

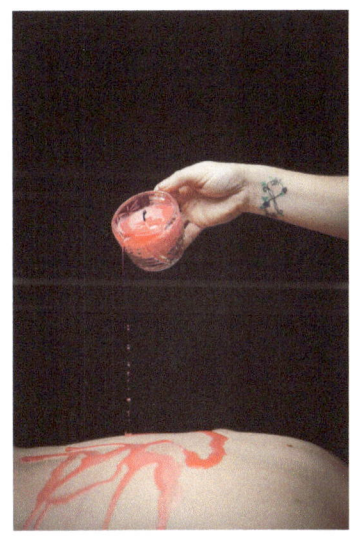

Be sure to always blow the flame out on a candle in a container before pouring. The flame directly on the glass can make it shatter leading to both burns and cuts.

The 7-Day religious candles (spiritual candles, saint candles, Jesus candles, player candles) are the go-to for wax play in the BDSM world. They are cheap and easy to use. They can either be burned or pre-melted directly in their containers.

Massage candles have very low melting points and are poured either in the hand or directly on the partner. Body heat is enough to keep the wax in liquid form, so it can then be rubbed into the skin. These candles can have a variety of ingredients that will be listed on the packaging. Some are made with a basic mix of soy, shea butter, almond oil, and essential oils.

Using massage candles that have color added is not recommended. The color will coat the skin and leave an unhealthy tinge. Purple might make the skin look bruised, sunburned, or bloody. Blue hypothermia? A yellow mango scented massage candle caused me to look jaundiced and I immediately needed to wash it off.

Tapers do need to keep their shape so additives that harden the wax are necessary like Viagra for candles, so it doesn't droop. Thinner tapers require more and as a result will have a higher melting point.

Tapers are popular with riggers because the candles can be secured in the ropes to drip on their rope bottoms. Several erotic play candles making companies make rigger sticks specifically for this use.

In-between the two are votives and pillars. Votives are about the size of bathroom Dixie cups, can be made with lower melting point soy wax. I prefer votives because of the low temperature wax and they are easy for me to transport.

As you can see, there are many different types of wax and candles which can make for a varied wax scene.

Types of Candles Quick Reference

Type of Candle	Characteristics
tealights	small candles in thin metal or plastic cups very little wax cups get hot
votives	small, squat candle sits independently made with variety of different waxes
pillar	tall, usually cylindrical in shape
taper	tall thinner than pillars usually cylindrical often has additives to help the candle keep its shape
container	most often in jars, cups, or milk pitchers softer wax doesn't need hardeners to help keep their shape
massage candles	soft wax and oil mixture melts quickly to be poured on partner and used to massage

Prep

Depending on how extensive your plans for your wax scenes are will determine the preparations you make. I have wrapped entire tables in plastic down to the floor as well as three feet up a wall.

> *"Tinder, it looks like you're setting up a kill room."*

Many things can be used to cover the area underneath the wax bottom and don't have to cost a lot of money. You might just use a lightweight plastic shower curtain or a cheap plastic tablecloth from a dollar store. When you're done any mess can be easily wrapped up in the plastic and tossed in the trash. Having a heavy-duty shower curtain on the floor below a raised surface can handle heels and be reused.

A cloth barrier between the skin and the plastic helps prevent the need to pull plastic away from delicate body parts. An example would be using a hand towel underneath someone's junk. Unless you are a sadist. In which case, just keep on doing what you do.

Plates or small trays for the candles helps protect the surface underneath and make it easier to move the candles around as needed They can also be used to take the used wax to the trash can.

Always be considerate of your hosts if you are not in your own home and make sure you do clean up after yourself.

Old hand towels can be used for wiping hands as the scene progresses. A wet one can be used for safety.

At minimum, wax bottoms should shower and wash their bits and pieces carefully. Wax play is a close contact kink, so a basic level of cleanliness is appreciated. Also dripping wax into belly buttons can be fun but a big turn off if they are already filled with lint.

Some people will use oil on the skin to make the wax easier to scrape off. For some that's exactly why they don't use it. The most popular are mineral (baby oil), grapeseed oil, and coconut oil. Those prone to breakouts should use grapeseed instead of coconut. On a comedogenic rating scale from 0 to 5, grapeseed oil is rated as a one while coconut oil is rated as a five.[18] Exfoliating after a scene can help counteract coconut oil's pore clogging effects.

Your scene will run more smoothly if you have all your supplies for the scene on hand and ready to go.

Prep - Quick List

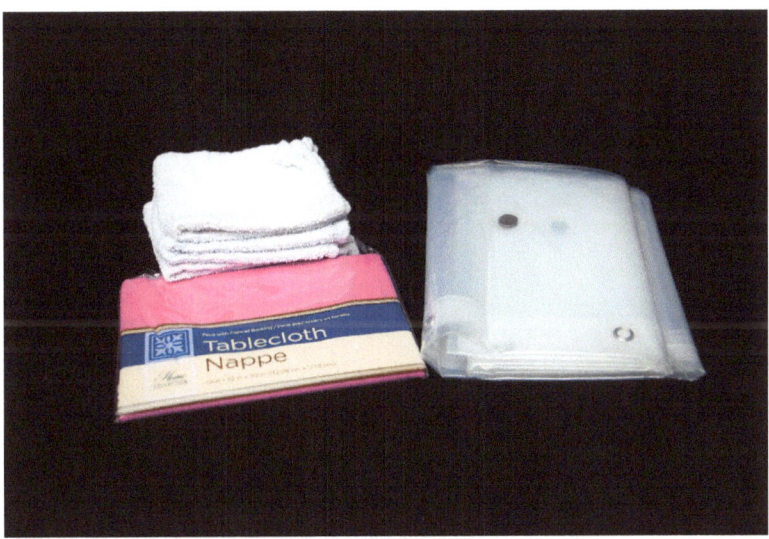

- Plastic shower curtain or tablecloth
- Old sheets, towels, or cloth tablecloth
- Oil (coconut, grapeseed, mineral, or baby oil)
- A stack of old small towels
- Plate or small tray

Style

There are many ways to play with wax. Even after all the scenes I've done, I still learn new techniques all the time.

Safety reminder: no matter how you incorporate wax into your scene, always test your wax on yourself first.

Drip, drip, drip

Votives, pillars, and tapers can be easier to transport and faster to use. They can be used like standard candles or even more sadistically melted using a crème brûlée torch.

Start by holding the candle about 18 inches above the skin. The distance allows time for the wax to cool before it hits. Depending on how your partner reacts, the candle can be raised or lowered to change the temperature.

How you hold the candle also affects the temperature. If the wax feels too hot, or not hot enough, try holding the candle at different angles. Allowing the wax to drip down the side of the candle will allow it to cool compared to the wax dripping directly from the flame.

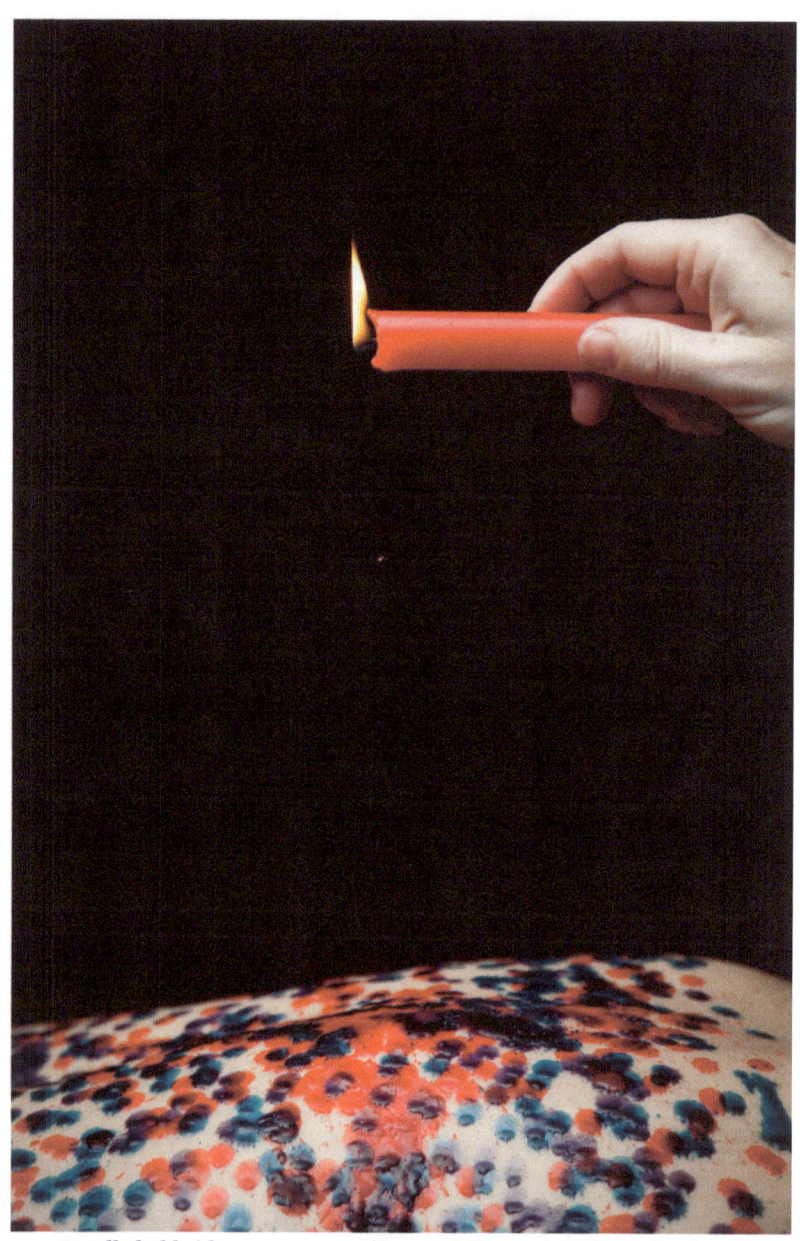

Candle held sideways means the wax falls straight from the flame.

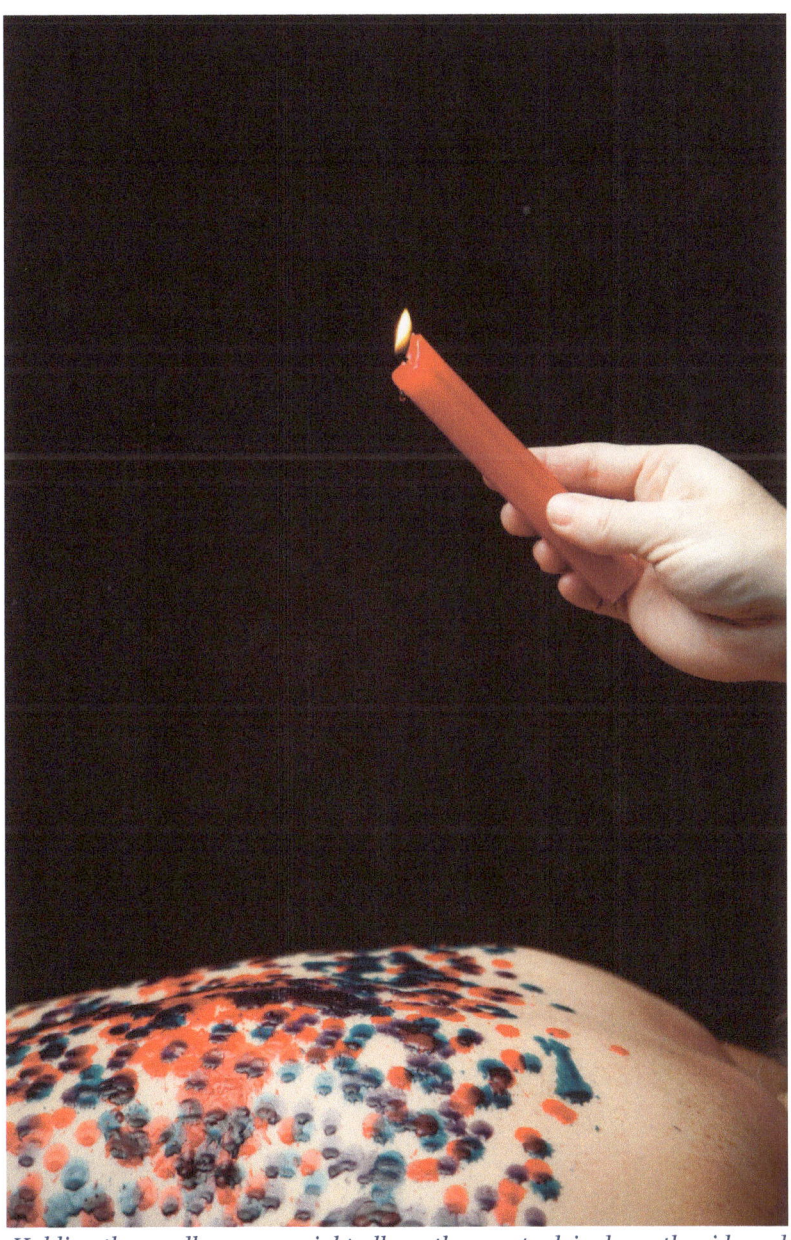

Holding the candle more upright allows the wax to drip down the side and cool more.

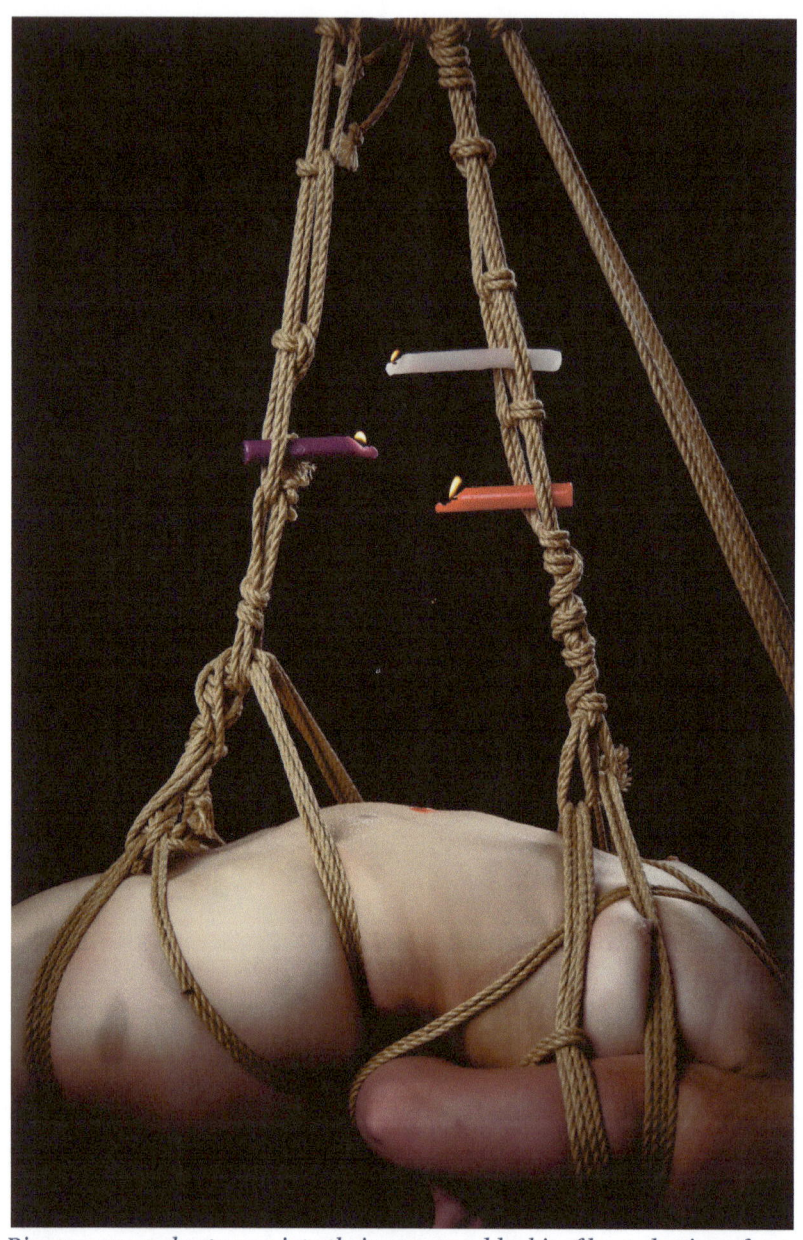
Riggers can wedge tapers into their rope to add a bit of heated, stingy fun to their scenes. The right position can create a slow, torturous sensation for the bottom.

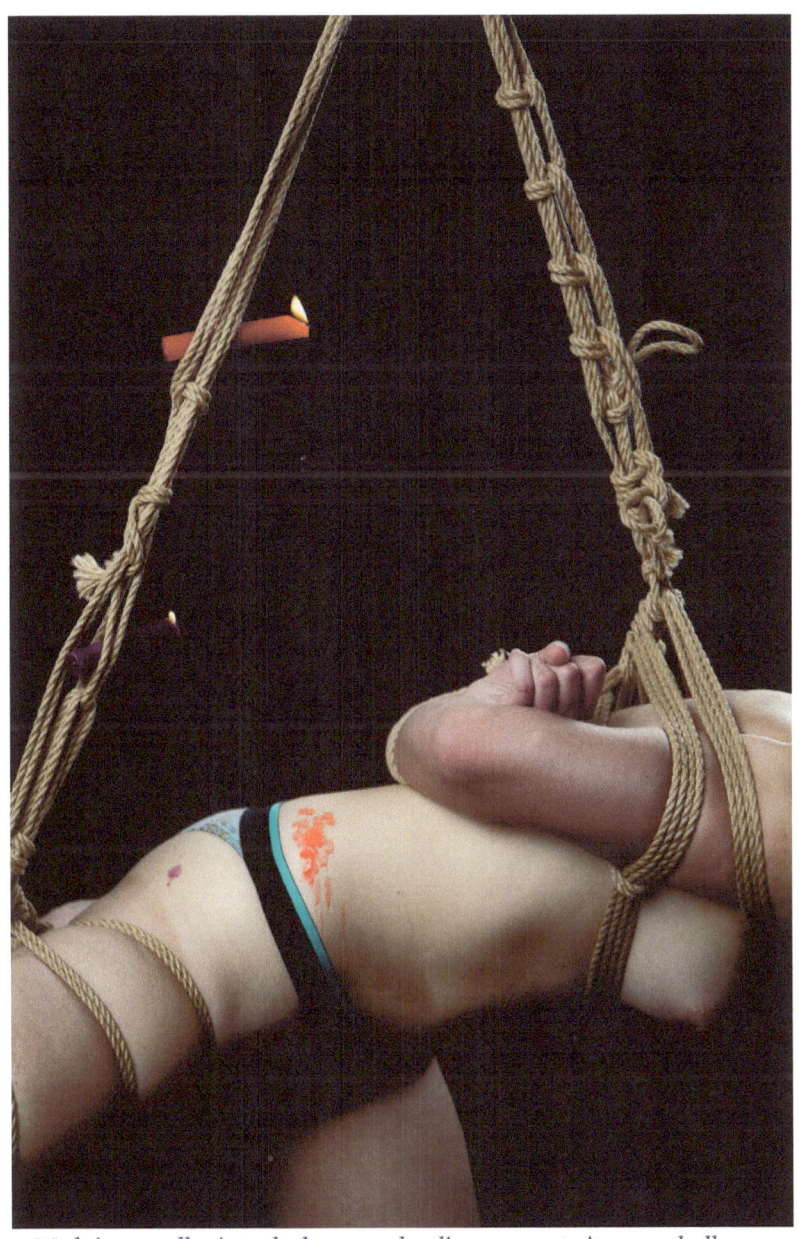

Wedging candles into the knots and uplines presents its own challenges though. Be sure the candle is secure enough not to flip or fall. Also check that the rope isn't directly above the flame.

Making a Splash

Wax play does not require an open flame. Heat can be applied in different ways. While the wax does take longer to melt in containers and requires more equipment, the temperature of the wax is more easily controlled.

Crock pots and electric skillets make for good wax warmers.

The religious candles can be melted directly in the crock pot filled with water and turned on high. Using containers small enough to fit in the crock pot with the lid on will melt the wax faster. Erlenmeyer flasks are great since their flat bottoms have more contact with the heating source. Shot glasses allow the wax to melt quickly as well.

Do not put cold glass containers into hot water. The sudden change of temperature could crack or shatter the glass.

The wax can be melted directly in the crock pot like a paraffin bath and, using a ladle, poured directly onto the body.

In my experiences and opinion, the right temperature hovers around 135°F. Wax can start congealing at 120°F and I personally have not yet come across anyone who finds above 155°F enjoyable.

Candle warmers are easy to transport but can heat the wax to over 165°F. A meat thermometer helps keep track of the temperature, so someone won't burn their partner. It doesn't take long for the wax to cool down to the right temperature after removing it from the heat source.

A paraffin bath is specifically made for spa paraffin, such as Therabath brand, which has a lower melting point. It can be ladled on and used as a base coat to protect the skin when hotter wax is used. It can also be used to anchor candles when the they are set directly onto the body. Make sure you are using the correct paraffin. Candle making paraffin won't melt completely, has a much different feel to it, can burn the skin, and is very difficult to clean up.

Accents to the fun

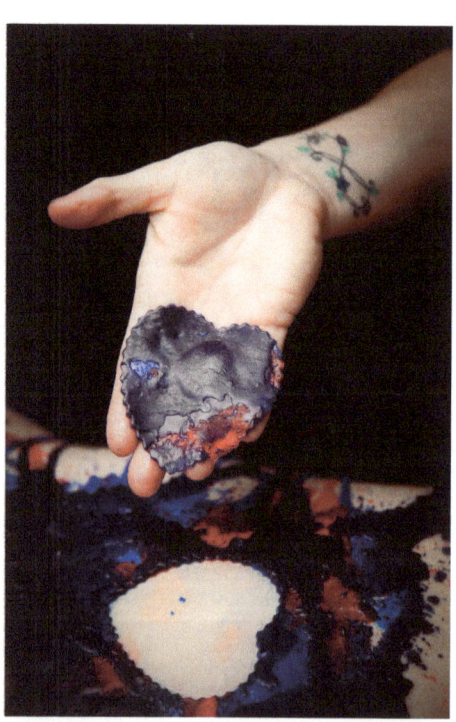

Lay down ribbon before pouring the wax over it. When you lift the ribbon, the wax peels off in strips too.

Cookie cutters are fun in many aspects. Shapes can be made after pouring the wax on the skin. Wax can also be poured or dripped into the cookie cutter directly. Some have been lucky enough to go home with their wax 'cookies'. Greasing them with some oil first will help the wax slide out easier.

Try pushing the cookie cutters into their skin and then start scraping the wax off.

Combining ice with wax bring a nice contrast to the scene. The wax can be poured over the ice like scotch on the rocks or an ice cube can be run over the wax after you have dripped/poured it
onto to the skin. Depending on your partner's limits, any body part can be used. A crotchful of cold ice and hot wax is a great way to keep someone's attention.

Extra Sensitive

Anyone with an extra sensitive partner can make accommodations. Wait longer for the wax to cool when using any wax in containers. Use a spoon to drizzle it like chocolate on a dessert. Pour the wax into your hand, smack their ass, and leave a waxy handprint. If the wax starts to congeal, scoop it out and smear it on. It'll be messy but a friend of mine says to just make it messier.

Some Like It Hot

Of course there are also options to make the scene more intense. One of which is to choose a more delicate location. The genitals and nipples are very sensitive but there are some other creative parts of the body that someone might not expect. The feet are calloused but the area between the toes aren't and might get more of a reaction.

Always make sure you receive consent to touch and apply wax in any of these locations.

Start the scene with some impact or fire cupping. Anything that brings blood to the surface of the skin will make it more sensitive.

Leave the candle dripping in the same place to build up heat and intensity. This works well when combining wax with suspension. Wedge the candle in the rope, sit back, and enjoy.

Use a crème brûlée or cigar torch lighter to melt the wax faster and bring the wax to a much higher temperature before it drops directly from the flame to the body.

There are as many different styles of wax play as there are people in the community. Mix and match these styles to make your own or come up with something brand new.

Removal

People

The scene doesn't stop with applying the wax. It can be just as much fun to remove it and you can be just as creative.

Most kinksters use knives for wax removal. Knives can be so wonderfully versatile. Running the tips through the wax can break it into pieces as well as get around and into the small areas like the belly button, nipples, or against the neck.

A pocket knife with a blunt edge can work as can a serrated dinner knife. Individually packaged knives from fast food restaurants are great for kinksters who don't want to gunk up their personal knives or feel it's unhygienic.

Hold the knife at an angle and push against the skin gently.

Dulling down the edges is important if you haven't also negotiated a cutting scene. You aren't performing surgery and again unless you have already negotiated it, you aren't looking to remove any skin tags.

Make sure you also dull down the tip. When using the blade around curves like the breast, neck, sides, and thighs, dragging the tip can scratch the skin and draw blood as well.

It is possible to make the edge too dull. The edge needs to be able to slide between the wax and skin to be effective.

If you are iffy when it comes to using a knife on your partner, and having confidence is important when you play with sharp things, you can always try wooden or plastic knives. Using a plastic gift card is safer and still gives the partner a good scratchy feeling.

Of course, knives aren't the only tool you can use for removing wax. There are so many other toys with nice sharp edges. Cookie cutters don't just make and cut out shapes but can also be dragged over the skin.

There are also wire cheese slicers, wartenberg wheels, shedding blades, icing spatulas, putty knives, fishing line, and flea combs.

These items very in degrees of effectiveness and can take up a lot of space in your play bag. I love my shedding blade, but it is relatively large and sharp. As a result, it is a pain to pack.

If oil was used and enough wax was dripped or poured, hands might just be enough to slide underneath the wax and lift big sheets at a time. I have sometimes been able to lift mold of nipples or belly button. I still have a mold of my crotch from a scene done in mid-2017. For me it's a keepsake and reminder of that wonderful night.

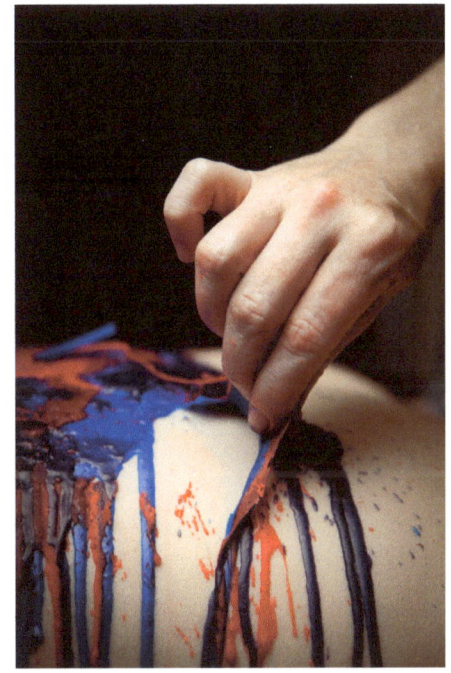

The skin stays warm from the wax. As a result, the wax stays pliable and easy to peel away from the skin.

Baby wipes, paper towels, and old towels will help get the remnants off, so everyone can cuddle up without continuing to trail wax flakes around. Showering should only occur when there is minute amount of wax left since it can clog pipes in a manner Drano cannot fix.

If wax gets into the bottom's hair, a fine-tooth comb will be the best, most effective way to remove most of it. One can also wrap the section of hair with a paper towels and use a hair dryer to melt the wax transferring it to the paper towel. In my own experience, combing the wax with a fine-tooth comb before shampooing and conditioning twice with hot water worked well enough. There are many complicated ways to remove wax from hair but more often than not, simpler is better.

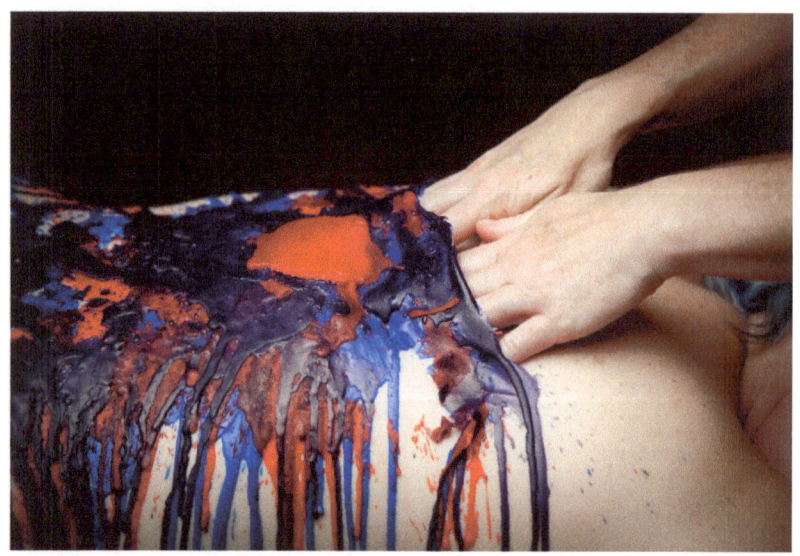

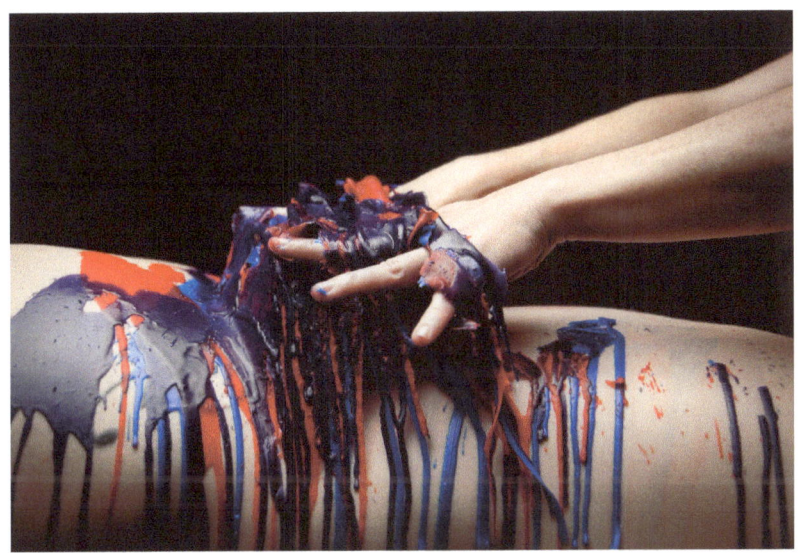

Things

If you drip wax on a piece of clothing, put it in the freezer. Gently scrape as much of the wax out of the fabric using a plastic pan scraper, which won't tug or pull at the individual fibers. Sandwich the fabric between a few paper towels or a paper bag and run an iron on low over it. The wax will melt out of the clothing and be absorbed into the paper.

With cloth that is too delicate for an iron, hold it over a bowl and run boiling water through the fabric instead.

Rubbing alcohol is a degreaser found in hair sprays and hand sanitizers. It can help remove candle stains and works well because it evaporates very quickly. Just use a cotton ball to dab the alcohol directly onto the stain. Always check the fabric colorfastness in a hidden area first. Never use on acetate, rayon, wool, or silk.

Some store-bought stain removers and laundry detergents are effective at removing candle wax. The type of wax used will determine the best detergent and spot remover.

There is a point where you must decide how much effort you want to expend on the process and whether it can even be rescued at all. Something cheap or old? Into the trash it can go. A Tom Ford original? Well shit. What were you thinking? Throwing a $150 Calvin Klein dress into the washing machine can be a risk that may or may not pay off.

If you don't wish to deal with the hassle, both you and your partner could just play naked which is a great way to play no matter the motivation.

A plastic scraper can also get wax off tables, kitchen counters, and non-carpeted flooring. If you need to get the wax out of the wood grain, use a hair dryer and paper towel by alternating using the blow dryer and dabbing or rubbing the surface with the paper towel. Rub with the grain and not against it. This method could also be used to get wax out of carpet.

As always be considerate of your host's space if you are not playing at home and clean up after yourself.

Aftercare

After the scene, the body should be visually and tactilely inspected for allergic reactions or burns. Feel the skin for any hot patches and note any excessively red spots.

Inform your partner of any areas to watch more closely as blisters may take time to form.

Don't pop any blisters that may be found. Cover them with a bandage to protect them from rubbing against clothes.

Drink lots of water. Temperature play can really make someone sweat and everyone will need to replenish those lost fluids.

Cuddling on the couch, having sex, or even helping each other shower off the remnants, what the rest of aftercare entails depends on you.

Wax play can be an amazing connection between people. For me, the touch and intensity are very strong motivations. I can connect with many people in my community and I am grateful for all those who trusted me over the few short years.

About TinderHella

It wasn't long after joining the community that TinderHella discovered her passion for wax play. A scene from the Madonna movie Body of Evidence had piqued her interest. Since then she has become fully obsessed with all aspects of wax play from making candles, to creating elaborate pictures, to giving fun and informative demos.

But the pictures aren't the center of her scenes. Her connection with her partner is. Without the flow of energy between them, Tinder says the scene feels empty and that she feels drained.

Fortunately, with the number of scenes she has done overall, those scenes are few and far between. For the most part, she thinks wax is fun and loves taking people with her on that journey. She is happy to pass on the knowledge she's gained over the relatively short period of time she has been gathering it.

Thanks to her obsessive curiosity about all things wax, Tinder has a lot of info stored up in that brain that she wishes to share. She is not an expert. She does not have all the answers and is only one of many resources. Consult others. Ask questions. Never stop learning.

Wax Candles Vendors

Links here do not equate to a product endorsement of any kind. Some only sell through their Fetlife.com profiles, which requires a Fetlife account to access. Thank you to the Candle Wax group on Fet for posting this list. Each site and vendor was checked for broken links and recent activity.

US:

- Fet: TinderHella (SURPRISE!) - Hella Good House of Wax on Etsy
- Fet: PainfullyKnk
- Agreeable Agony
- Fet: Bears_Kitty - Bear Things
- Fet: Kitsune_Candles
- Fet: ShellnCrossbones
- MSW Candles on Etsy
- Fet: LeatherTykeProducts - LeatherTykeProducts.com
- Panda's Candles - on Etsy

UK:

- The Bondage Man
- Trussed UK
- Kandles By Kitten - on Etsy

Canadian Shipping only:

- Fet: KushielsGirl - Kinked Wood

Australia:

- Red Rigger Candles on Etsy

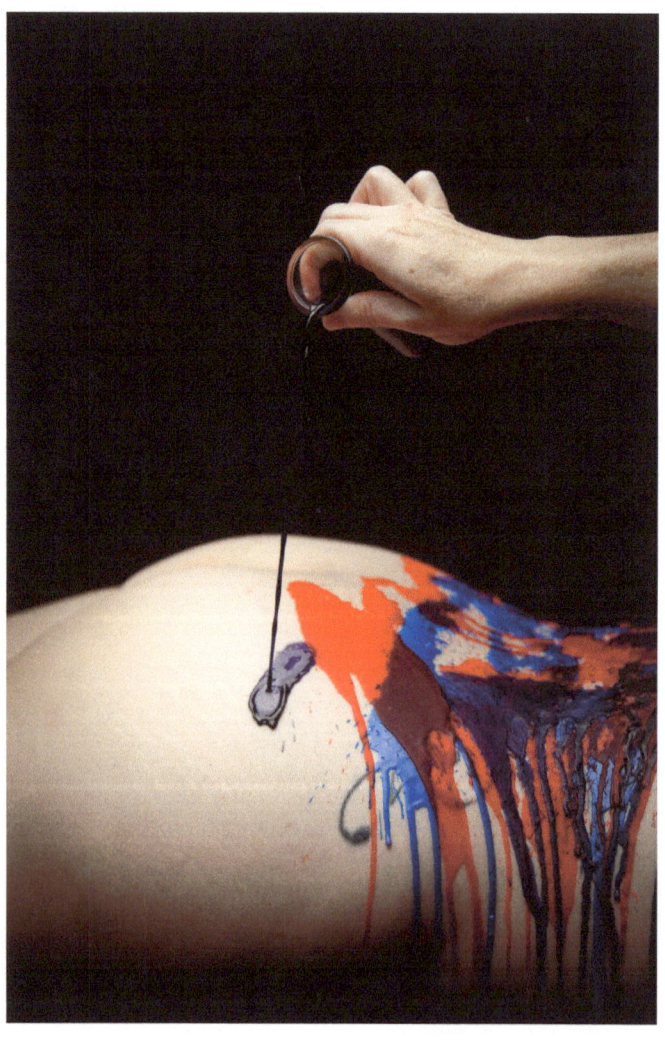

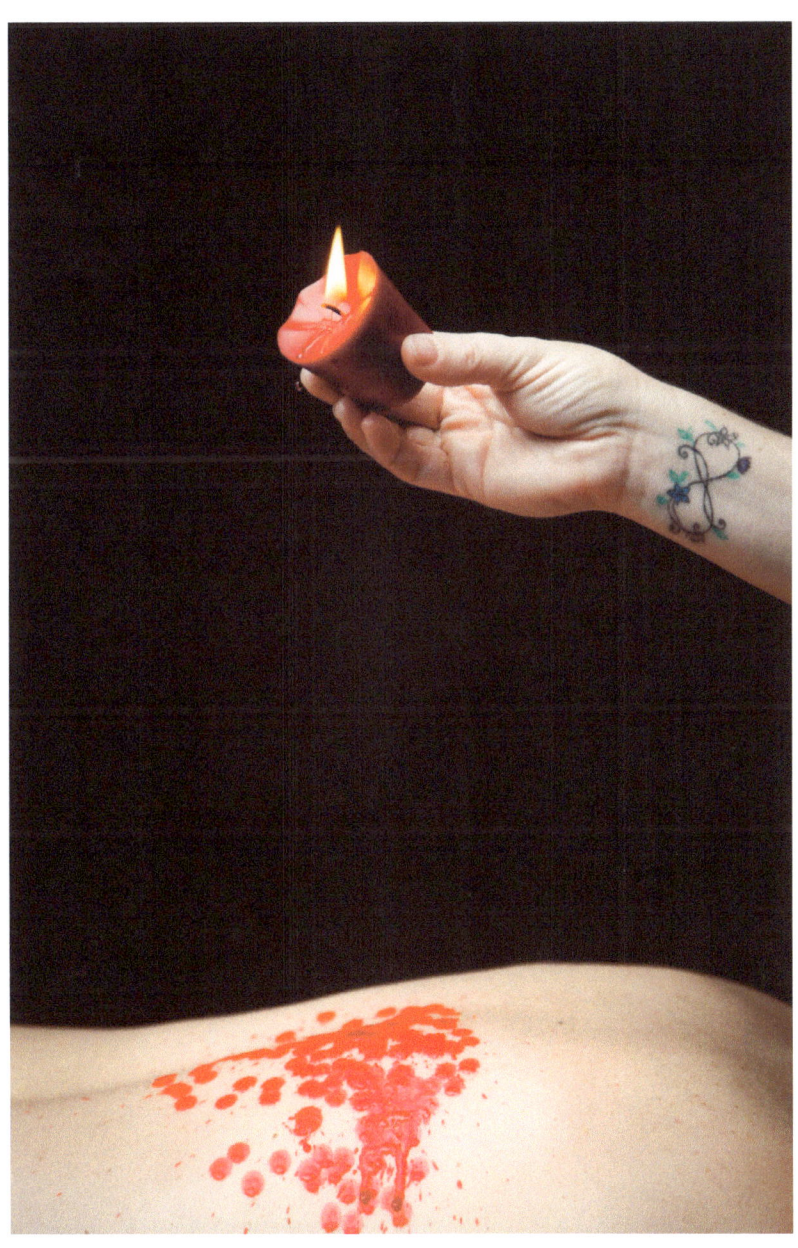

Endnotes

[1] American Burn Association Scald Injury - Prevention Educator's Guide - http://ameriburn.org/wp-content/uploads/2017/04/scaldinjuryeducatorsguide.pdf

[2] National Candle Association - Fire Safety & Candles - http://candles.org/fire-safety-candles/

[3] Association European Candle Makers - Raw materials and candles production processes - https://europecandles.org/raw-materials-and-candles-production-processes

[4] Chemical Book – Paraffin Wax - http://www.chemicalbook.com/ChemicalProductProperty_EN_CB2854418.htm

[5] The National Institute for Occupational Safety and Health (NIOSH) – Paraffin Wax - https://www.cdc.gov/niosh/ipcsneng/neng1457.html

[6] Mother Earth Living – The Ancient History of Beeswax - https://www.motherearthliving.com/health-and-wellness/natural-beauty/the-ancient-history-of-beeswax-zeoz1506zdeb

[7] Fisher Scientific - Material Safety Data Sheet – Beeswax - https://fscimage.fishersci.com/msds/02556.htm

[8] Your Candle Store – Additives - https://yourcandlestore.wordpress.com/additives/

[9] Pure Integrity Soy Candles - http://www.pureintegrity.com/best-scented-candle.html

[10] How to Make Candles - Stearic acid (stearin) - http://www.howtomakecandles.info/cm_article.asp?ID=ADDIT0003

[11] Thermodynamics Research Center, NIST Boulder Laboratories, M. Frenkel director, "Thermodynamics Source Database" in **NIST Chemistry WebBook, NIST Standard Reference Database Number 69**, Eds. P.J. Linstrom and W.G. Mallard, National Institute of Standards and Technology, Gaithersburg MD, 20899, doi:10.18434/T4D303, (retrieved August 15, 2018). https://webbook.nist.gov/cgi/cbook.cgi?ID=C57114&Units=SI&Type=TFREEZE#TFREEZE

[12] NIST Standard Reference Database 69: *NIST Chemistry WebBook* - https://webbook.nist.gov/cgi/cbook.cgi?ID=C555431&Mask=FFFF&Units=SI

[13] How to Make Candles - Vybar - http://www.howtomakecandles.info/cm_article.asp?ID=ADDIT0002

[14] Rustic Escentuals – All About Gel - https://rusticescentuals.com/All-About-Gel.html

[15] Infinite Flame Magick Shoppe – The Truth About Gel Candles - http://www.infiniteflame.com/gelcandleinfo.htm

[16] EHow – How to Make Metallic Colored Candles - https://www.ehow.com/how_5580262_make-metallic-colored-candles.html

[17] Earth Guild - Using Metallic Candle Color to coat candles - http://www.earthguild.com/products/riff/rmetalcc.htm

[18] Beneficial Botanicals – Comedogenic Ratings - https://www.beneficialbotanicals.com/comedogenic-rating/

www.ingramcontent.com/pod-product-compliance
Lightning Source LLC
Chambersburg PA
CBHW041508010526
44118CB00006B/192